MALDIVES
A Nation of Islands

Contents

Published by Media Transasia Limited for Department of Tourism
Male', Republic of Maldives.

Photography by Alberto Cassio

ISBN 962-7024-03-1

MALE'

Male', the capital, is and always has been the seat of government in the Maldives and the home of the intellectual elite. Economically, its structure is different to the other islands – for, if the islands depend on Male' for all their trading and administration, Male' depends on the islands for *its livelihood.*

The impression is of a bustling, lively, prosperous town. The unpaved coral streets and the intricate leafy lanes throng with people and with bicycles, cars, motorcycles and trucks.

For islanders and travellers alike, Male' is the crossroads, the main trading depot and the only contact with the outside world. All manner of goods are brought here from the farthest-flung atolls, and all manner of imports pass through it on their way outwards.

Male' is divided into four traditional wards : Henveyru, Galolu, Machchangoli and Maafannu.

The President's residence, or *Mulee-Aage,* built in 1913 to a design by Maldivian and Ceylonese architects, is a short distance, opposite the Friday Mosque, or *Hukuru Miskiy,* which dates from 1656 and contains accounts, carved on wooden plaques, of the conversion of the Maldives to Islam. The courtyard of the mosque houses the tombstones of past rulers. The minaret, or *Munnaaru,* built in 1675, is a distinctive, drum-shaped tower from where the people are summoned to prayers five times a day. Every Friday, thousands congregate here to offer their prayers.

Most government offices, situated either on the seafront's busy Marine Drive or behind this on the elegant Ameer Ahmad Magu, are found in Henveyru, while Maafannu, which occupies almost the entire western half of Male' provides with its tall, shady trees pleasant surroundings for a large section of the residents of the capital.

NISHAAN

CRESCENT XIV
M-1/13. MARINE DRIVE

Male', the capital island-town gives the impression of being a bustling, lively, prosperous town — unpaved coral streets and dirt lanes throng with people, bicycles, motorcycles and increasingly, cars. Roadside shops do brisk business and at the docks there's always sacks waiting to be loaded.

Bicycles are ubiquitous in Male'. Indeed they are the popular mode of transport and overflowing cycle stands adjoining office blocks attest to this. Wood is an important element in Maldivian life, largely used in boat-building, construction and as firewood.

GEOGRAPHY

The Maldives' International Airport on the island of Hulule, directly adjacent to Male' and which was commissioned in November 1981, has opened the Maldives to the outside world. Regular flights operate between Male' and Colombo, and Male' and Trivandrum in South India, while wide-bodied charters carry tourists directly from a number of destinations in Europe to Male'. There is no regular sea passage, but Maldivian cargo vessels will provide passage to and from Colombo at a low price.

Seen from the air, the atolls and islands form the most beautiful patterns against the deep blue of the Indian Ocean. The Maldivian atolls are a classic example of their kind : in fact, the English word "atoll" was derived from the Maldivian *atholhu.*

The atolls form a long, narrow chain that is strung along a length of 512 miles roughly north to south, and which measures 81 miles across at its greatest width. The atolls rise from a common plateau, a long-dead volcanic landmass, and are separated from each other by deep channels, some easy to navigate, some with strong currents and uncharted reefs. The enclosure reefs to each atoll contain openings for boats travelling between the atolls, but many of these are suitable only for the traditional Maldivian sailing boat, the *dhoni.*

The islands are formed from coral layers rising sharply from the plateau. Most are situated close to the atoll enclosure reef and vary in size from patches of coral or small sandbanks, to real islands — some are still in the process of forming. The longest of the islands is Gan, in Laamu Atoll, and is 4.5 miles long. Male', the capital, occupies an island barely one mile long on the east side of Kaafu Atoll. Most other islands are less than a mile long.

Because they are based on coral, the islands are flat, the highest point rarely being more than six feet above sea level. However, they are protected from the elements by the atoll reefs, and rarely suffer major storms. The water table is naturally high in all the islands, and some have small freshwater lakes. All the

The islands have been formed by layers of coral rising sharply from the sea bed plateau. Most are situated close to the atoll enclosure reef and vary in size from patches of coral or small sandbanks to large islands – some are still in the process of forming.

older islands, where a layer of soil has formed on top of the coral base from accumulated animal and vegetable matter through the millenia, are covered with tropical vegetation, typically coconut trees towering above dense shrubs.

The climate, which is hot and humid, is determined by the monsoons. The southwest monsoon comes at the end of April with a steady westerly surface wind that generally continues until November. The northeast monsoon, from December to March, is the driest season of the year. The annual average rainfall on Male' is around 84 inches, and the mean temperature varies little throughout the year, averaging 86 degrees Fahrenheit.

There are very few animals indigenous to the Maldives, but the islands are a haven for seabirds. The most spectacular wildlife is to be found underwater, where rainbow-hued tropical fish teem amongst the multi-coloured coral reefs, along with crustaceans, turtles, shells and fantastic seaweed growths which combine to form a silent, spellbinding world.

The islands are grouped into 26 natural atolls, but for purposes of administration they are divided into 19 atolls with the capital, Male', forming the twentieth division. Each atoll consists of a number of inhabited, and a greater number of uninhabited islands. The total number of islands is 1190, while inhabited islands number 200.

The islands abound in marine life and undersea exists a spectacular world of coral and colourful tropical fish. Shoals of rainbow-hued fish live in this twilight world of crustaceans, turtles, shells and fantastic seaweed.

Coral formations encircling islands and sugar white beaches set in emerald waters. As the depth of the water increases, the sea turns from clear light blue to green and finally deep blue as the ground drops away to meet the ocean floor.
Overleaf: There are very few animals indigenous to the Maldives but the islands are a haven for seabirds.

Maldivian pistols on display at the Male' museum along with intricately decorated handy-boxes earlier used by the ruling family.

Right: one of the earliest surviving examples of writing on parchment – in this case, the land deeds for a mosque. With increasingly close contact with the Arab world and India, a distinctive Maldivian language emerged known as Dhivehi, based on Elu, an offshoot of Sanskrit

HISTORY

The earliest history of the Maldives is lost in antiquity. Legend has it that long ago an Aryan prince was becalmed on one of the islands, where he found an aboriginal race who welcomed him and, finding he was of royal blood, crowned him King of the Maldives.

Whether the prince, who is popularly known as Koimala, is mythical or not, it seems certain that the islands were first settled by Aryan immigrants from India and Ceylon. Till very recently it was believed that the first settlements took place around the 4th or 5th century BC, but the latest archaeological findings suggest that the islands had been inhabited as early as 1500 BC.

However, trading contacts with the Arabs and Persians, East Africa and Madagascar, Malaysia and Indonesia, have left their imprint on the people and culture of the Maldives. Increasingly close contact with the Arab world, and with India over many centuries, brought about important changes in the language and script of the Maldivians, and eventually a distinctive Maldivian language evolved, known as Dhivehi. Based on Elu, an offshoot of Sanskrit, it has strong elements of both Arabic and Hindustani, and is spoken more or less uniformly throughout the atolls.

The oldest form of Dhivehi can be seen inscribed on gravestones and on copper plates and slabs of stone found in some of the mosques. Of these, the best preserved are the copper plates known as *Loamaafaanu,* the earliest of which dates back to the late twelfth century (1195-96) and the latest to the mid-fourteenth century (1356-57). They are written in the ancient Maldivian script *Eveyla,* which itself gradually gave way to what is known as *Dhives Akuru,* the characters of which are simpler and more uniform. *Dhives Akuru* is found in common use in the mid-sixteenth century. At about the same time, a new script evolved called *Thaana.* Unlike the two former scripts, the writing of *Thaana* is from right to left – probably to accommodate the many Arabic words then in everyday use.

Owing to its comparative isolation, the Maldives

had few visitors over the centuries apart from the traders. Some of the well-known writers and travellers of the second to the sixth centuries AD make fleeting references to the islands, but then there appears to be a gap until the ninth century when Arab travellers began to leave more detailed accounts. However, it was not until the fourteenth century, and the arrival of the great Moroccan traveller Ibn Batuta, that we have our first full account. He landed early in the year 1343 AD and stayed for eighteen months, working in the service of the ruler. His account observes that the Maldivians were engaged in regular trade with Arabia, India and China in dried fish, coconuts, coir and cowries, besides ambergris and tortoise-shells.

There are only two other well-known full accounts of the Maldives from then until the 1880s : one by the French mariner Francois Pyrard, shipwrecked on the islands in the seventeenth century; and the other by British naval officers Lieutenants Christopher and Powell in the 1830s.

Pyrard's tale is a remarkable combination of adventure and meticulous scholarship. His ship, the *Corbin,* ran onto a reef in July 1602. Almost from the first, Pyrard obtained exceptional treatment from the Maldivians. For four years he was allowed to travel amongst the islands, and even allowed to trade. Then in February 1607 a raiding party from Chittagong arrived at Male', intent on salvaging the *Corbin's* cannon. Pyrard and his three remaining companions were taken to India by the invaders.

He reached Paris in 1611, and his account was published there in the same year. Apart from telling of the voyage, the wreck, the various fates of the crew members and the author's own experiences, Pyrard's book gives a description of the Maldive Islands, details of the religion, manners and customs of the people, the government and the court, and of trade and commerce.

The Arabs, in their travels in the Indian Ocean, had soon discovered the Maldives, which lay directly on the route between Malacca and China. The most significant contribution that the Arabs made to the Maldives was Islam : it was in the year 1153 AD that the Sultan officially accepted Islam and declared it the religion of his domain. Prior to this, Buddhism was prevalent in the islands, and a number of ruined temples bear witness to this fact.

With the exception of a 15-year period in the sixteenth century, when the Portuguese ruled the country from Goa, the Maldives has remained an independent sovereign state throughout its history. The past rulers can be divided into a number of dynasties, and the names and accomplishments of various Sultans – and sometimes Sultanas – who ruled with varying degrees of wisdom through the ages, are listed in the State Chronicle, known as ''Tarikh'' of Hasan Tajuddin.

The ruler at the time of the advent of Islam was Koimala, who was re-named Sultan Mohammed ibn Abdullah, after conversion to the new faith. He reigned for 25 years in all, thirteen of them after his conversion. Many a legend surrounds this famous king, who was the founder of the Theemuge Dynasty, and who ruled a

unified Maldives from Male'. The Tarikh gives one account of the coming of Islam, which is related in H C P Bell's work :

"The Almighty God, desiring to free the natives from their slough of ignorance, idolatory, and unbelief, and to lead them into the right path, inspired the Shaikh Yusuf Shams-ud-din of Tabriz, the most pious saint of the age 'whose knowledge was as deep as the ocean,' to visit the Maldives. The shaikh there conjured the islanders to become Muslims, but failed until he had roused them by displaying miraculous powers, such as the raising of a colossal *Jinni,* 'whose head almost reached the sky.' Then the king and all the inhabitants became Muhammadans....The conversion took place on the twelfth day of Rabi-ul-Akhir, *Anno Hijrae* 548 (1153 AD)."

Ibn Batuta relates another version, which assigns the credit for the conversion to Islam to Abul-Barakat Yusuf, the Berber, who exorcised a *Jinni* that monthly demanded the sacrifice of a virgin at the idol temple in Male'; the saint took the intended victim's place and recited the Quran throughout the night—the *Jinni* never came again. Both of these tales of conversion would indicate a background of animism, but the date seems to be accurate.

The Theemuge Dynasty lasted for 235 years and produced 26 rulers. The Hilali Dynasty came next, with 29 rulers over a period of 170 years. The final Sultan in this line was Ali VI, who fell in a vain attempt to defend his country against the Portuguese. Known to history as Ali the Martyr, he reigned for only two-and-half

Top left and centre: tombs of the former rulers of the Maldives at the Male' Friday Mosque and copper plates (Loamaafaanu) bearing the earliest and best preserved examples of Dhivehi script.
Above: old map of the Maldives and an ancient Maldivian shield.

XLIII.—1881.
THE
MÁLDIVE ISLANDS:
AN ACCOUNT OF
THE PHYSICAL FEATURES, CLIMATE, HISTORY,
INHABITANTS, PRODUCTIONS,
AND TRADE.
By H. C. P. BELL, Esq.,
Ceylon Civil Service.
Ordered by His Excellency the Governor to be Printed.
Colombo:
FRANK LUKER, ACTING GOVERNMENT PRINTER, CEYLON.
Presented
TO
HIS HIGHNESS
MUHAMMAD SHAMS-UD-DÍN ISKANDAR,
Sultan of the Maldive Islands,
BY
H. C. P. BELL,
Ceylon Civil Service (Retired).
THE MÁLDIVE ISLANDS:
1920.
BELL.

Facing page: H C P Bell's definitive survey of the Maldives published in the 1880s.

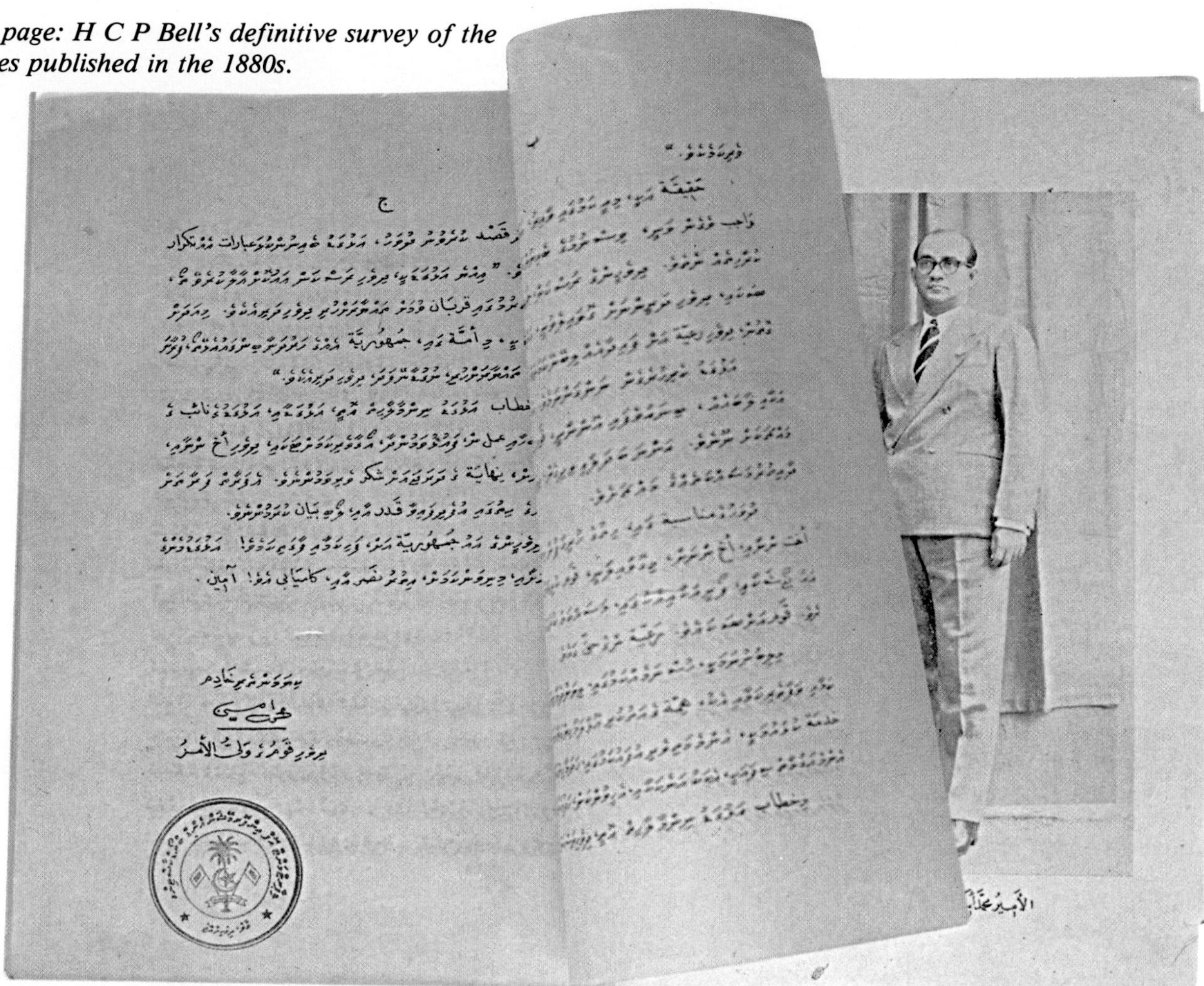

months; yet is considered to be, because of his martyrdom for the country, one of the greatest to occupy the throne of the Maldives.

The subjection of the Maldives by the Portuguese was bitterly resented, and the invaders found great difficulty in controlling the large number of islands spread out in seas dangerous to shipping, and with constant attacks by hostile Maldivians. Eventually, an uprising was led by three brothers from Utheem island in Thiladhunmathi Uthuru. The eldest of the three was captured and beheaded, but the other two brothers led an attack against the Portuguese stronghold in Male', slew the governor and wiped out the entire garrison. The Portuguese were never to return. The older of the two brothers, Mohamed Thakurufaan the Great, came to the throne in the year 1573, founding the Utheem Dynasty. He is regarded as the greatest of Maldivian national heroes, and his almost legendary exploits are still celebrated in story and song.

This dynasty ruled for 127 years, producing 12 rulers. Then followed the brief Isdhoo Dynasty, which, with its two rulers, ruled for only five years, and led on to the Dhiyamigili Dynasty, which lasted for 55 years. Its third and final ruler had been on the throne less than three years when, in the year 1752, a raiding party from the Malabar coast of India landed on Male', destroyed the palace and sent the Sultan into exile; he never returned. The Malabar raiders remained on Male' for only a few weeks before they were repelled by Maldivian forces led by Ghazi Hassan Izzuddeen, who founded the Huraage Dynasty, which lasted until the Maldives became a republic in 1968.

The period between the liberation of the country from the Portuguese and the repelling of the Malabars was a tumultuous one for the Maldivians, who fought thirteen wars to preserve their independence during this time. After the Malabar episode, the Maldivians began to cultivate relations with Ceylon, or Sri Lanka, as it is called now. First records of diplomatic missions from the Maldives to Ceylon go back to 1645, but now an alliance was formed that continued throughout Ceylon's Dutch and then British colonial periods.

An agreement was formalised in 1887, when the Maldives accepted British suzerainty in return for military protection. In practice, Britain did not interfere with the internal affairs of the Maldives to any noticeable degree, and there was no British governor or representative stationed in the Maldives at any time; all Maldivian foreign affairs were conducted through Colombo. The ingenuity of the Maldivians had again managed to find a way of keeping their own world to themselves, for Britain was all-powerful in the Indian Ocean, and what the Maldives really wanted was unobstructed relations with Ceylon which supplied all their needs.

The Maldives too has succeeded in remaining entirely Maldivian – it is the only country in or around the Indian Ocean where there is no distinct Indian community, language or religion. That this small nation situated so close to the subcontinent and at a very strategic position, was able to maintain its own identity as an independent nation fully intact is a magnificent tribute to the ingenuity and far-sightedness of its forefathers.

Mr. Maumoon Abdul Gayoom became President of the Republic of Maldives in 1978.

When former President, Mr. Ibrahim Nasir, declined nomination for a new term of office that year, Mr. Gayoom was nominated by the Citizens' Majlis to become the next President. He polled a record 92.9 percent in the public referendum and assumed office on 11th November.

Mr. Gayoom entered government service in 1971 and served in a number of posts before becoming the permanent representative of the Maldives at the United Nations in 1976. He was recalled a year later and was appointed Minister of Transport.

In both style and substance, President Gayoom's administration represents a major shift in political and economic direction. In a policy statement to the Majlis in February 1979, he committed himself to a more open government, to greater freedom of the press, and to running the government according to the principles of modern democracy. The decision-making process has been decentralized, with greater reliance on consultation within the cabinet and increased powers for both the Citizens' Majlis, and the judiciary.

Mr. Gayoom, born to a middle-class family in Male' in 1937, was educated at Al-Azhar University of Egypt where he obtained an MA in Islamic studies. He also studied Law and Philosophy there, and did a post-graduate course at the American University of Cairo. He was a lecturer in Islamic Law and Philosophy at Ahmadu Bello University in Nigeria from 1969 to 1971.

He is married to Nasreena Ibrahim (33) who takes a keen interest in all his activities. The Gayooms have four children, Dunya and Yumna (twin girls aged (13), Faris (12) and Ghassan (3)

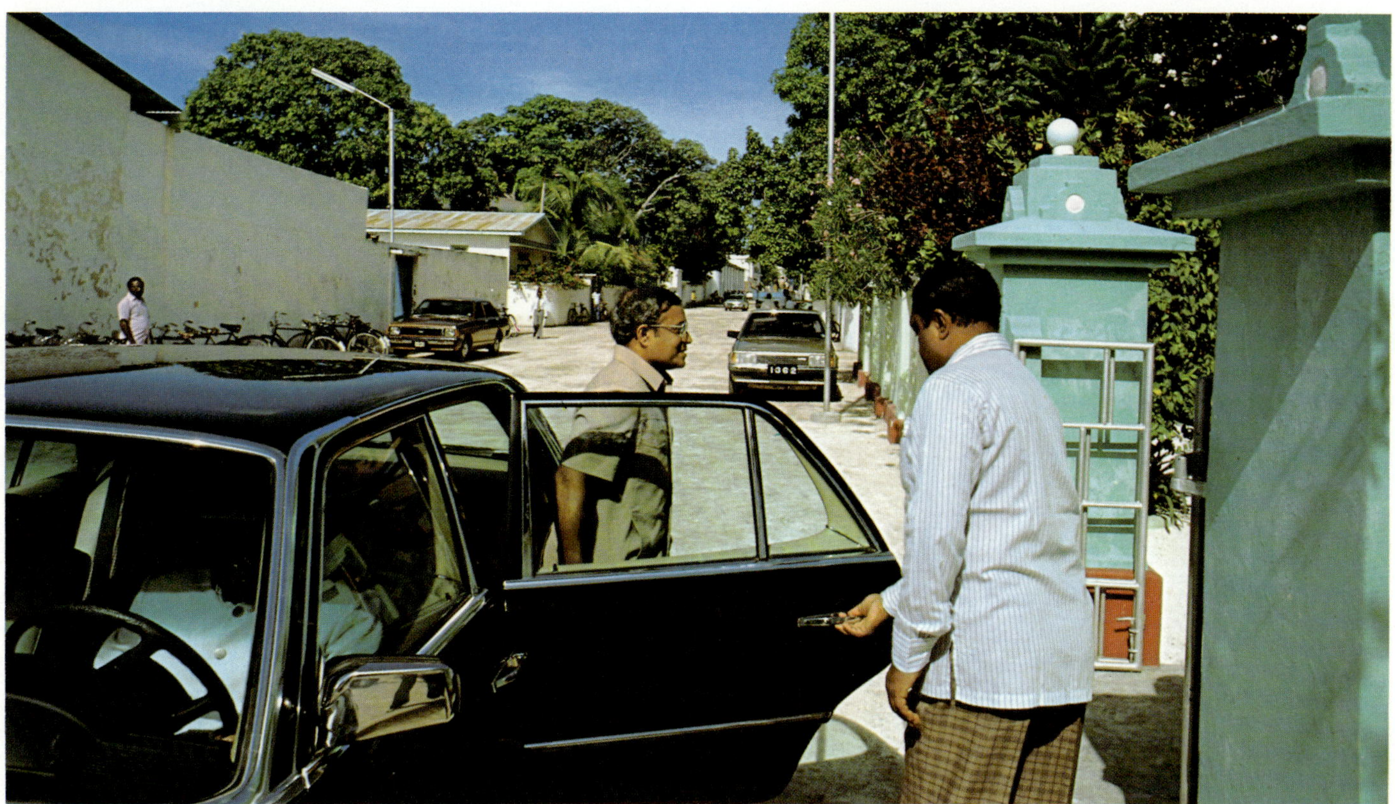

THE CONSTITUTION

The Maldives is a composite, sovereign and independent republic. Its capital is Male'. The official religion is Islam, and the language Dhivehi.

The first written constitution of the Maldives was proclaimed in 1932. But a deeper study of the evolution and development of the system of government and administration in the Maldives would show that there have been unwritten constitutional principles of long-standing which were accepted by the people in the form of time-honoured customs.

Koimala, the first king to embrace Islam in the Maldives assumed the Islamic title of Sultan. All subsequent kings and queens were known as Sultans and Sultanas. The post of Sultan was not hereditary; it was rare when a son succeeded his father to the throne purely as a matter of natural succession. There were systems of taxation, national defence, discharge of public duties and administration of justice. These were clearly defined by usage though not by written laws.

The earliest constitutional practices, as far as written evidence shows, were evolved in the period of the Male' Dynasty which ruled from 1141 to 1388 AD. They include the appointment of advisors to the Sultan, whereby the principle of consultation and people's participation in administration were established.

The reign of the Utheem Dynasty was a period of reform and organisation. The defence of the country was organised, an educational system was established and the high office of Sultan became an institution rather than a person. Tenets of democracy in the form of the consent of the ruled became more evident in the decisions of the Sultan. The next notable period of constitutional development was the era of the Hura Dynasty, as the power vested in the Sultan in earlier periods began to give way to the power of the Chief Minister.

The 47 years of rule by Sultan Muhammad Imaaduddin IV from 1835 to 1882 provided a long period of calm and relative stability. The Maldives by this time had contacts with the British Colonial Government through its representative in the region. This Sultan's long reign gave more power to the nobles known as "Bodun."

With the advice of the Bodun and the then protecting power, Britain, Sultan Muhammad Shamsuddin III proclaimed the first written Constitution in 1932 by which he volunteered to limit his powers. The Sultan and the Bodun obtained the advice of the British Government in the drafting of this Constitution. In 1934 Sultan Hassan Nuruddin became the first constitutionally elected Sultan. He ruled until 1942, when he resigned; and after a two-year period, during which the country was ruled by a council of regency, Abdul Majeed Didi was elected to become the next Sultan but he died before being coronated.

Over the next two decades or so, the Maldives progressed from a constitutional monarchy to a republic. A short-lived republican interim occured in 1953 when Amin Didi became the first president of the country, propounding nationalism and modernisation, but after seven months, internal troubles forced him to resign.

Under the last Sultan, Mohammed Farid Didi, Ibrahim Nasir became Prime Minister, and on 11 November 1968, the second republic was proclaimed, with Nasir as President. He ruled with an autocratic hand until 1978, when growing resentment prevented him from seeking a third term. He was succeeded by the present President, Maumoon Abdul Gayoom, who is committed to a more open form of government.

According to the present Constitution, the President is the head of state and the chief executive. He is nominated by the Citizens' Majlis (Parliament) and elected by a public referendum for a renewable term

وأمرهم
شورى
بينهم
1932
١٣٥١

of five years. He is also the Commander-in-Chief of the Armed Forces and the supreme authority to protect and propagate the religion of Islam in the country.

The Cabinet of Ministers comprises the President, Vice Presidents if any, heads of the Ministries and the Attorney-General. The President appoints the Ministers and terminates their appointments. A Minister may be questioned by the Citizens' Majlis regarding the administration of office assigned to him. If a "no confidence" motion is passed on a Minister by the Citizens' Majlis, he is required to inform the President of such a motion and resign immediately.

The Citizens' Majlis, which is the main legislative body in the country, comprises 48 members – two elected from each of the 19 atolls and Male', and eight presidential appointees. The Citizens' Majlis is elected for a five-year term. All laws except those that have to be passed by the Citizens' Special Majlis have to be passed by the Citizens' Majlis.

The Citizens' Special Majlis consists of the members of the Cabinet, members of the Citizens' Majlis, two members elected from Male', two members from each of the 19 atolls and eight members appointed by the President. If it becomes necessary to amend any part of the constitution or to add or delete an article, it has to be passed by a majority vote in the Citizens' Special Majlis. The power to summon the Citizens' Special Majlis rests solely with the President.

The administration of justice, according to the Constitution, shall be conducted by persons appointed by the President. In addition to the eight Courts in Male' there is an Island Court established in each of the inhabited islands. The High Court of Maldives, which is presided over by the Chief Justice, is the Court of Appeal.

The Constitution has no provision for local government. The islands are grouped into 19 administrative units called *atolls,* each one headed by an atoll chief, appointed by the President. Every inhabited island has a government-appointed island chief, or *khateeb,* who enforces law and order in the island. The atoll chiefs, together with the *khateebs,* are responsible for the maintenance of public order, the collection of statistics and the implementation of government policies.

The Maldives is a member of the Non-Aligned Movement and the Organisation of the Islamic Conference. It became a member of the Commonwealth in 1982. It has diplomatic relations with over fifty countries, and five of these have resident embassies in Male'.

RELIGION AND THE PEOPLE

Islam is the strength and backbone of Maldivian society, permeating as it does the entire educational system, for there is a strong tradition of Quranic scholarship at all levels. It is the religion of state, and every Maldivian is a Sunni Moslem; no other religion exists amongst Maldivian citizens. The faith is taken very seriously -- the law allows for no deviations in matters such as the Ramadhan fasting, drinking alcohol or eating pork. Prayers are conducted five times a day in all the mosques on every inhabited island.

Islam in the Maldives has, however, its own unique character, a delicate blend of tradition and modernity. The family is the basic unit of society; the male is the most respected member of the household -- yet women have never been kept in purdah. Their access to education is completely open; they participate freely in social activities and play an important role in the economic life of the islands, and on Male', where female employment in offices is plentiful and on the same pay-scale as men.

From their infancy, Maldivians are brought up to respect their elders. The inhabitants of each island form a closely-knit group, where everyone knows each other; for the majority of islands have a population of less than 1000. Social services, law and order, and investment decisions are the responsibility of the island community, directed by its headman - the island *khateeb,* and overall in each atoll, by the atoll chief.

The atolls, and some individual islands, are almost self-contained economic units, depending on the sea around them, as fishing is the main activity. Boys learn seamanship early, often going out on the fishing boats by the time they are 10 or 11 years old. The more sons a father can bring along on a boat, the bigger his share of the catch, for the fish are divided amongst the crew. The women and girls are the homemakers, also tending some of the crops and producing handicraft items. Unlike women elsewhere in the islands of the Indian Ocean, they do not market the fish caught by their menfolk.

Preceding pages: teaching the Quran at the school adjoining the Friday Mosque. Islam is the strength and backbone of Maldivian society and a strong tradition of Quranic scholarship exists at all levels. Above and right: vignettes of a people.

Male'island has a special vitality.

At work and at play.
Overleaf: A vital link with the outside world – the international airport and runway on Hulule island a few minutes by boat from Male'.

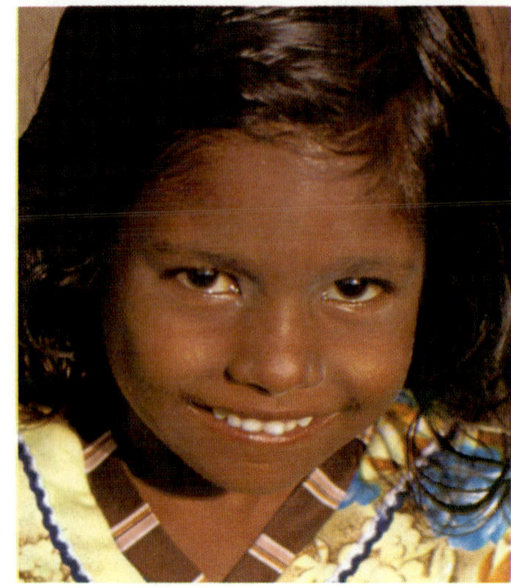

S14077

TRANSPORT & COMMUNICATIONS

Transport links both with the outside world and within the widely dispersed islands of the country are naturally of paramount importance.

Remoteness from the countries that supply the Maldives with essential imports would indicate that the country is highly vulnerable to any disruptions in shipping services, and that, as the country's main export, fresh fish, leaves via special collector vessels, cargo ship operators bringing imports to the Maldives would face the uneconomic prospect of returning with almost empty holds. However, with what now seems to have been remarkable foresight – for this was before the days of frozen fish exports – the Maldives established its own shipping line, Maldives Shipping Ltd (MSL), in 1966. The company evolved out of the old Maldives National Trading Corporation (Ceylon) Ltd, which had been established in 1948 and which operated ships between India, Burma, Ceylon and the Maldives. Starting off with two 2,500 tons vessels, MSL quickly increased its tonnage. Both administration and operations were originally based in Colombo, but in the mid-1970s, MSL's operational headquarters were shifted to Singapore and the administration to Bombay. Finally, when the new three-storey MSL office complex was commissioned in 1979, the major part of administration and operations was moved to Male', while maintenance of the fleet remained as a responsibility of the Singapore branch.

Although the initial purpose in acquiring ships was to ensure a cargo trânsport service to and from the Maldives, the fleet has expanded so much in recent years that the Maldives' imports and exports now represent only a tiny proportion of the fleet's total operations. The fleet now stands at around 35 vessels with a total tonnage of 265,000 deadweight.

The shipping industry has been a profitable one. Naturally, MSL has ploughed most of its profits back

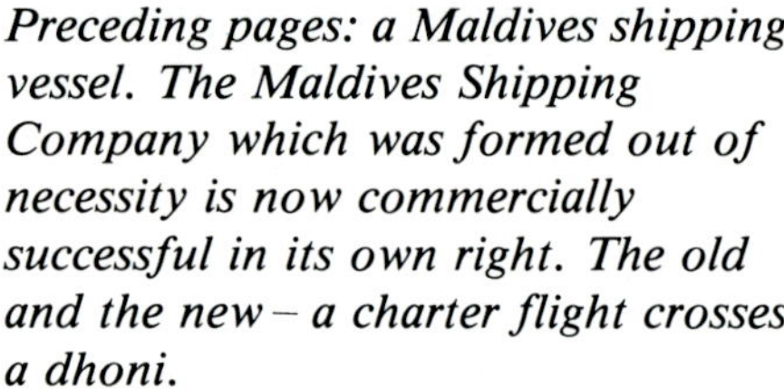

Preceding pages: a Maldives shipping vessel. The Maldives Shipping Company which was formed out of necessity is now commercially successful in its own right. The old and the new – a charter flight crosses a dhoni.
Above and right: winging through Maldivian skies and a powered boat – bringing the islands closer.
Centre: the traditional dhoni, which has evolved perfectly over the generations to suit the needs of sailing in Maldivian waters.
Far right: boat building is a vital industry.

into fleet expansion, but it still makes a significant contribution to the country's foreign exchange earnings. It is also an important employer, providing jobs for more than 1000 Maldivians.

The Male' Port offers only limited facilities for ocean-going traffic; there is no deepwater berth and imports are discharged by lighters, which are hauled by tugs to the wharf and off-loaded there by mobile cranes.

All inter-island traffic is by sea, except for Gan, which is a two-hour flight away by light aircraft. Traditionally, people and goods were transported between the islands on a friendly or barter basis. In recent years, the build-up of tourism and the mechanisation of fishing boats has brought considerable improvement to inter-island transport.

The graceful *dhoni,* the traditional Maldivian sailing boat, is mainly used for transport to the islands within an atoll, while the motorised version, or a larger mechanised boat, is used for inter-atoll transport. Most of this traffic between the atolls is in fact between Male' and individual atolls; the capital is still very much the focal point of the archipelago.

There are no regular schedules; journeys to the southern atolls may take a week because of the hazardous seas and consequent frequent night stops.

Communication between Male' and the atolls is through a network of HF transceivers, but telephone calls can be made from Male' to the main island of each atoll and vice versa via the Department of Posts and Telecommunications. Within each atoll communication between the island and also with boats is by walkie-talkie. A VHF radio telephone system links most of the tourist resort islands to Male'. External telecommunications are provided via a satellite earth station which is equipped with four channels and is capable of transmitting and receiving telex, telegraph, facsimile, and data traffic as well as with voice channels for international telephone calls. The satellite station is operated by Cable & Wireless under a lease arrangement with the Government.

Satellite stations, telecommunications, television and increasingly efficient air transport links are the backbone of the new developing Maldives.

FISHING

Fish is the mainstay of the Maldivian economy, accounting for nearly one-third of the gross domestic product and employing more than 40 percent of the workforce. In fact, outside of Male', fishing provides the main livelihood for the vast majority of the island population.

Fish are caught for home consumption, for sale in the domestic markets and for export. Not surprisingly, per capita consumption of fish in the Maldives is one of the highest in the world, and fish is the main source of protein for the inhabitants of the archipelago.

Skipjack is the main catch. Surface skipjack occur all year round outside the atoll reefs, while deep-sea tuna can be found in commercial quantities only for a period of two to six months a year. Other fish include varieties of bottom fish, shark, bait fish and lobster.

The Maldives is famous for a particular skipjack product which is known as ''Maldive Fish''; this is skipjack that has been boiled, salted, smoked and dried. Until 1972, it was the main export of the country -- Sri Lanka being the sole buyer. The foreign exchange crisis in Sri Lanka at that time caused them to limit their imports of ''Maldive Fish'', and the Government had to find other means of exporting fish. Agreements were entered into with various foreign companies which provided for the export of frozen fish.

The fish canning factory established in 1977 in Felivaru, about 76 miles to the north of Male', as a joint-venture with some Japanese companies, is now wholly owned and operated by the Maldives Government. The cannery exports canned skipjack and tuna to world markets.

The traditional fishing boat, the *dhoni,* began to give way to mechanised boats in the mid-1970s, as it was found that mechanised vessels were far more versatile and productive. A Government-sponsored credit scheme provides engines for applicants, and by the end of 1982, 1166 fishing boats had been mechanised. Mechanised vessels are also better suited to supply fresh

Out at dawn, searching for skipjack shoals. Bait is tossed into the ocean and as the morning progresses the catch is landed. Over 90 percent of the skipjack is caught by the pole and line method.

fish to the highly mobile collector vessels.

Besides mechanisation of fishing vessels, several other programmes aimed at the development of the fisheries sector have been embarked upon by the Government. These include projects for the provision of better collecting and storage facilities, better fuel distribution, repair and maintenance facilities for engines and additional marketing facilities.

Boat-building has long been an art in the Maldives. Expert carpenters in the country make the hulls of fishing boats out of coconut timber. The design evolved suited the local conditions perfectly, since fishing usually takes place at a distance of 15 to 20 miles from the outer reef.

Over 90 percent of the skipjack is caught by the pole and line method, by sailing and motorised boats, each with a crew of eight to thirteen. The remaining 10 percent comes from line fishing, either by trolling with small boats, long-lining or by hand-lining at night for reef fish.

The fisherman is looked upon as a very important member of the community, a view actively promoted by the Government with an annual "Fishermen's Day" (10 December), part of the endeavour to persuade young men to enter the industry after they have finished their schooling.

Fishing is the mainstay of the Maldivian economy providing one third of the gross domestic product and employing more than 40 percent of the workforce.
Centre: 'Maldives Fish' drying in the sun.

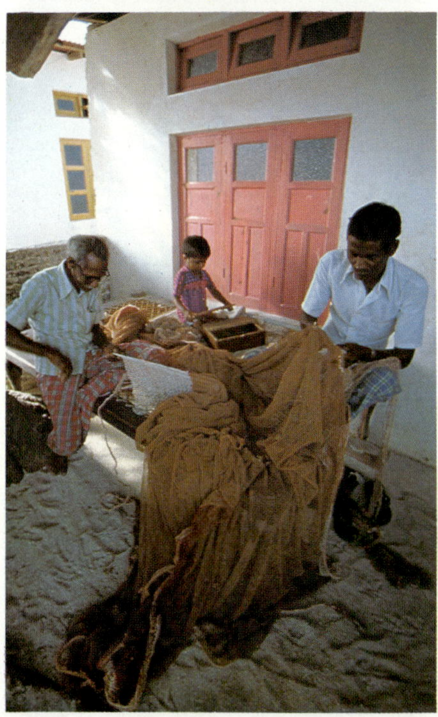

TOURISM

With limited potential for industrial development, but with a unique, unspoiled beauty, it was perhaps natural that the Maldives should turn to tourism as a source of foreign exchange earnings. And in little more than ten years, the tourist industry has leapt from nothing, to more than one-tenth of the gross national product, accounting for some three-fifths of visible export receipts.

To the tourist in search of an exotic holiday destination, the Maldives offer a Robinson Crusoe setting, with lofty coconut palms, jungle foliage, white peaceful beaches and a warm lagoon where snorkelling or diving will instantly reveal a wonderful undersea world.

It was with this potential in mind that the Maldivian tourist industry was established, and for effective promotion of the industry, the Government set up the Department of Tourism which is responsible for supervising, co-ordinating and maintaining the standard of tourist services in the country. A number of small, uninhabited islands were selected and resorts built up on them; in keeping with national policy, all the resorts are Maldivian-owned, some of them being leased to the resort operators.

There are, at present, 48 island resorts and five hotels in the country, with a bed capacity of over 4300. Each resort is a small, self-contained community. Great care has gone into preserving the desert island atmosphere. The rooms are generally built to look like local housing, with coral for the walls and palm leaves for the roofing. Restaurants, bars and other facilities are in a central complex, built to a similar design. Facilities are very modern – each resort has its own generators, water supply, radio-telephone, a small harbour or mooring and its own motorboats to transport guests to Male', to the airport or to other islands.

Most of the tourist arrivals are from Western Europe – some 85 percent on average, with the majority of these being West German, Italian, French and Swedish. Most come via a tour agency on a package arrangement. A valid passport or travel document and an international certificate of innoculation against cholera (if coming from countries where cholera is

endemic) are the only documents required for entry. All foreigners, on arrival, are given a 30-day stay permit.

There are no foreign exchange restrictions. All major currencies can be exchanged at banks, authorised money changers and in all the tourist resorts. The Maldivian currency, the Rufiyaa, has to be used for all transactions within the country. However, reconversion of Rufiyaa to US dollars can be done at banks or at the airport. There is a duty free shop at the airport fully stocked with watches, cameras, electronic equipment, cigarettes, perfumes, etc.

Being a 100 percent Muslim country, visitors are not permitted to bring in liquor. However, a variety of alcoholic beverages are freely available in the tourist resorts and hotels.

Tourist resorts are an important source of employment for Maldivians -- they are in well-paid jobs and are learning new skills. There is very little encroachment by tourists upon the culture of the Maldivians, as the resorts are all on islands close to Male' with very little real communication between the visitors and the general population of the islands. There are no Maldivians permanently living on any of the resort islands.

Herwarth Voigtmann

Herwarth Voigtmann

HIEDE PRINTING T.SHIRTS
OUR SERVICE
OUVENIRS TARTARUGA
Antique & Style
DASISTDAS
BILLIGSTE
ESCHAEFT IN.MALE
ANDERES

EDUCATION

Education in the Maldives falls into three separate categories. The main system of schooling countrywide is through the traditional Quranic schools, or *makthabs,* which are spread across the entire chain of atolls, and which constitute the backbone of the Maldivian educational system. These privately-run *makthabs* must be given credit for the very high level of adult literacy throughout the islands – around 82 percent, remarkable for its uniformity across age groups and sex – for most of the *makthabs* teach the young to read and write Dhivehi and Arabic and to do simple arithmetic.

However, the *makthabs* are designed to impart only the basics of schooling, and consequently actual educational achievement in them is low. A modern national curriculum was needed, and for this purpose the Dhivehi-medium system has recently been designed. This modern curriculum is taught in the Atolls Education Centres, of which 11 have been opened. These schools are larger than the *makthabs* and their teaching scope is far broader – the curriculum has nine subjects, namely environmental studies, Islam, Dhivehi language, English, mathematics, fine arts, physical education, handwriting, and Quran. Here, as in the *makthabs,* all tuition is in Dhivehi; English is taught as a second language. One of the problems facing these schools at present is the lack of qualified teachers.

There are in Male' a number of English-medium schools, both government and private. These schools prepare students for GCE "O" Level examinations of the University of London. The curriculum taught at the

In recent years the Government has made it a priority to upgrade the educational system with a view to achieving three main objectives – universal primary education, increased output to meet manpower needs and an improved teacher training system.

Science Education Centre, which is run by the government, enables the students to sit for the London GCE "A" Level examinations. There are, in addition, a fair number of private schools in Male'.

The English-medium schools, which are largely staffed by expatriates, have been successful in reducing the number of Maldivians who go abroad, to Sri Lanka or India, for schooling. However, there is no higher education in the Maldives, and those desiring a university education have to travel abroad.

In recent years, the Government has made it a priority to upgrade the educational system with a view to achieving three main objectives : firstly, to attain the goal of universal primary education; secondly, to increase the output of secondary and vocational schools to meet the country's increasing manpower needs; and thirdly, to upgrade the teacher training system to help meet the needs of the first two objectives.

Programmes for attaining these goals are operating at all levels throughout the atolls. In addition, the English-medium schools in Male' are being expanded and a Vocational Training Centre in Male' is proving successful in producing skilled workers.

The health infrastructure is based on the primary health care approach. Health care is provided at 21 health centres which cover all the atolls. Each of these centres has at its disposal a health launch which is used both for routine services and for emergency transportation.

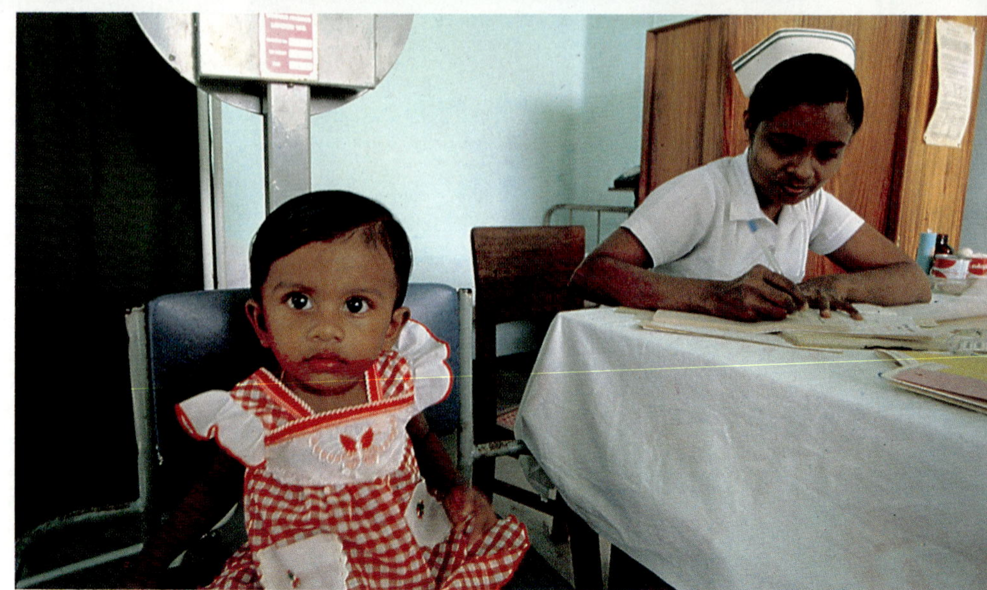

HEALTH

The health infrastructure of the Maldives is based on the primary health care approach. All health posts are linked with each other under referral arrangement.

Villages in the islands are served by peripheral health workers known as family health workers. Their main task is to provide preventive services, in addition to rendering minor curative services.

At the atoll level, health services are centralised at health centres, where a community health worker is posted. The services of health centres cover all the atolls. Further, each of the 21 health centres in the Republic has at its disposal a health launch which is used both for routine services and for emergency transportation.

In 1982, the first of the proposed four regional hospitals began to serve the northern quarter of the country. The Central Hospital in Male' has the highest level of health facilities in the country and it functions as the nucleus of the referral health system.

The Government has embarked upon many other horizontal health programmes, namely a leprosy and TB control programme, a malaria eradication programme, filaria control programme and provision of safe drinking water and sanitary facilities. However, there is still much to be achieved. Life expectancy, though, has increased from 46.5 years (1977) to 51.5 years at present, and there has also been a marked improvement in the infant mortality rate, which has fallen from 120 per 1000 live births to 77 per 1000 live births. The major threat to the life of infants and young children is the frequent epidemics of diarrhoea and other similar diseases that can be prevented with better sanitation.

There is still an acute shortage of health personnel, though cadres of health workers are being trained at the Allied Health Services Training Centre to its full capacity.

AGRICULTURE

Although fishing is the main activity of the people of the islands, there are some islands where conditions are good for the cultivation of crops and where agriculture takes precedence over fishing.

The soil in general is young and vigorous; it is shallow, consisting of a sandy loam with a top layer containing varying quantities of humus. However, most of the soil is poor in water-retaining capacity, and is highly alkaline due to an excess of calcium from the basic coral rock.

There are no hills, mountains or rivers in the Maldives, and all field crops are raised on natural rainfall during the southwest monsoon season. Water is also available from the underground watertable which lies not too far below the surface; some islands have ponds or small lakes.

Coconut is the most extensively grown crop throughout the country and constitutes an important part in the Maldivian diet. Coconut timber is used for boat building as well as for construction of houses. Coconut palm is known as "Dhivehi Ruh" in Maldivian language, which means "the Maldivian palm", indicating the tremendous value it has to the practical life of the people. Breadfruit is also grown in all inhabited islands and is extensively used as food. The Government is giving high priority to the rehabilitation of coconut trees everywhere in the archipelago – every citizen is being encouraged to plant at least one coconut tree a year.

Crop cultivation is of the shift type, and very little inorganic fertiliser is used. Planting is mainly confined to the southwest monsoon season; the ground is prepared for planting at the end of April, and seeds are sown after the first rains. Harvesting is carried out three months later.

Finger millets and Italian foxtail millets are the two most widely grown crops throughout the Maldives. Sweet potatoes are grown on a fairly wide scale in the south and in some parts of the north, while cassava is grown as a field crop in many parts of the south. In the low-lying swampy areas found in some southern islands, taro is grown throughout the year. Maize, sorghum and bajara are also grown as field crops in many islands. Several other kinds of tubers are grown in house compounds. Green chillies and small red onions are grown on a fairly large scale throughout the Maldives, and cucumbers, beans, cabbages, pumpkins, ridge-gourds, bitter-gourds, brinjals and drumsticks are also grown in some of the islands.

Cultivation of watermelons, especially in Thoddoo in Ari Atoll, brings in ready cash to the farmers because of its proximity to the Male' market. Watermelons are grown widely in the north too. Breadfruits, bananas and screwpine are widely grown in almost all the islands, and mangoes, lemons, pomegranates, star apples, custard apples, sapodillas, wood apples, papayas, guavas and jujubes are mostly grown in house compounds.

The flourishing garments factory on Gan island.

GAN ISLAND

When the British closed their military base in Ceylon and moved in 1956 to Gan, the southernmost island in the Maldivian archipelago, job opportunities were created for the people of Addu Atoll. At its peak the British staging post employed some 1,200 workers, many of them skilled or semi-skilled, having been trained on the base. The island and its close neighbours prospered. Then in the mid-1970s came Britain's east of Suez policy which involved the withdrawal of all military forces from east of Egypt. The Gan base was closed in 1976, leaving the maintenance workers to migrate from the island and settle in nearby islands or atolls, or move to Male'. Many, with their training and proficiency in English, found employment on the resort islands.

The British left behind an extensive infrastructure that the Government found could be used in a key role in its regional development plan for the southern atolls – an infrastructure that included an excellent airstrip, port facilities, bulk fuel storage area, a powerhouse, freshwater and sewerage facilities, and the only road system outside of Male'. There are also more than 300 buildings of good quality typical of an RAF base, including residential quarters, fully equipped kitchens, cold stores, maintenance shops and leisure facilities.

The Government set up the Addu Development Authority with representatives from several ministries, and promoted the potential of the island and its facilities to foreign investment concerns. The result, so far, has been two-fold: a small holiday resort has been created out of some of the buildings, and also two highly productive garment factories began to operate in another section of the RAF complex. Once again Gan, which could so easily have become something of a ghost island, is a busy and productive place.